Imagir

Dream, was published by Anvil in 1985. This was followed by
The Secret Ministry (2001) and *Tenderness* (2004), both winners in
the Poetry Business pamphlet competition. *Tenderness* was also a
Poetry Book Society pamphlet choice.

His most recent collection *Keeping Time*, published by Salt, was
a Poetry Book Society recommendation for Winter 2008. This
new collection reprints the poems he wishes to keep from *The
Interrupted Dream*, some in different versions, along with twenty
poems previously uncollected in book form.

Also by Tim Dooley

Keeping Time (Salt, 2008)

Imagined Rooms

by

TIM DOOLEY

Tim Dooley.

*for Ann
with all good wishes
and good wishes
with your writing.
Tim x.*

SALT

CAMBRIDGE

PUBLISHED BY SALT PUBLISHING
14a High Street, Fulbourn, Cambridge CB21 5DH

© Tim Dooley 2010

Salt Publishing 2010

Printed and bound in the United Kingdom by Lightning Source UK Ltd

Typeset in Swift 9.5 / 13

ISBN 978 1 84471 770 5 paperback

1 3 5 7 9 8 6 4 2

for my family

Contents

Acknowledgements

Some of these poems appeared previously in the following magazines: *Ambit, Aquarius, Brittle Star, Cracked Lookingglass, Dog, Encounter, Green Lines, Green River Review* (USA), *North, New Statesman, nthposition, Numbers, Oxford Poetry, Perfect Bound, Poetry Durham, Poetry London Newsletter, Poetry Review, Poetry Wales, Siting Fires, Smith's Knoll, Southern Review* (USA), *Stroud Festival Poetry, Swansea Review. Times Literary Supplement, Tribune* — and in the pamphlets *The Secret Ministry* and *Tenderness* published by Smith Doorstop.

Thirty-five poems first appeared in *The Interrupted Dream*, published by Anvil Press in 1985 and now out of print. Thanks are due to Peter Jay and Peter Sansom for their early support, to many friends and editors for their comments over the years on individual poems, and to Todd Swift for his helpful comments on this selection.

The used surfaces of things, the wear that hands give to them . . . lend a curious attractiveness to the reality of the world. In them one sees the confused impurity of the human condition: the amassing of material, use and misuse of substance, footprint and fingerprint, leaving all made things marked by man inside and out.

Let our poetry be like them corroded by the hand's obligations, steeped in sweat and smoke, smelling of lilies and urine, stained by the work we live by. A poetry impure as the clothing we wear, or our bodies stained with soup or shame—our wrinkles, nightwakings, dreams; declarations of loathing and love; loyalties, denials and doubts; affirmations of faith and payments of taxes.

— *after* Pablo Neruda

A Part of the Main

A figure in a one-man boat
is pulling from his seine
fish that are strange to us.

On handkerchiefs of land
grow plantains, peppers fruit.

He steers between these fields
watching water shake itself
like a tall haze of sky.

The shining evening spins ahead:
his empty market tray,

or ice in a long glass of rum.
The tapir-driven taxis pass.
Men talk of bat and ball.

I am reading essays
for the overseas exam.

Through the poorly-puttied window
close wooden fences lean
like the walls of a shanty town.

The script lies open
on a small metal desk.

Mr. Persaud writing.
He wants to take a post
in some other, foreign country.

Poor prospects, rigidity,
Botched new developments.

He hopes for wealth, smart buildings
and: 'if I walk by a lake
with a girlfriend, no-one would talk'.

In my lakeless suburb
this back view of a house:

A figure in a lighted room
is reading on lined paper
words that are strange to him.

An Edward Hopper figure
in the static placeless night.

A clothed figure held up by light,
in the night where the world turns
and home is abolished.

Wondering what it would be like
in another, foreign country.

The zig-zag fire escapes,
fresh coffee, pretzels,
the rattling Legendary El.

Someone else's map invades
the starless blank through which we move.

We wear imported clothes,
eat fresh exotic fruit.
This news I hear—the Cortes

at gunpoint on all fours—
is local and is real.

Griefs pin-prick the night to form
reflecting the reclaimed land
we steer through with our days,

joined by some work or hope,
a message from another country

something glimpsed rocking
in the prow of a fisherman's boat,
wrapped in a coloured magazine.

We had to bring it along
so nothing would be strange to us.

Homefinding

If you find the new place, and when you've climbed
the stairs, unpacked each case and closed with care
each unfamiliar door, perhaps you'll stare
through these clean windows or, later, leaning
on the desk, you'll turn your head and say, 'I'm
glad we chose this place and glad I'm leaving
where I was before. The walls look older
here. Back then I hated walls. I thought they
kept all life outside and it was colder
when they curled around me. I kept away
from rooms before, but now so much has changed.
I like that chair; those flowers you've arranged.'

The new place is like that. It stuns us by
its size. We didn't think that warmth would flow
through pipes like that and make no sound. The high
ceilings are light, unstained and even. No
breeze disturbs a curtain, even less
your tired face, your rest. I'm sure you'll find
the place quite soon and hope that you won't mind
when you arrive, my asking the address.

Level Crossing

Who are the crazed ecologists
conserving dust in corners of our room?

Pity is in association for the microbe.
Appetite is browning like a steak.

We home to ancient manners; cigarettes
are finger-rolled. Billiard balls collide,

on contact crash down mushrooms, slide
into a hole. Beer's hopped, hand-pumped,

and downed where old men's cheeks
are local colour, fields are sown.

Tractors with searchlights tear at earth.
Wild geese and waders know the times of trains.

The cars will queue at the level crossing.
The railwayman will drag the gates.

In five years' time you stand him drinks
and hear of his arthritic hip.

Alfoxden 1798 (Problems in Criticism)

                                   'Query: Are
the male and female flowers on separate trees?'
'The day cold'
                —and, returning from her visit
to Holford Woods, Wordsworth's sister
                            (called exquisite
by his discerning friend, the noted critic)
                                wrote these
words inside her journal.

                               'On separate trees.'
What could she mean describing hollies so? Is it
a symbol born from melancholic whim
                            that she's
just left for Will to pick at?
                        I'll accept with ease
Whatever explanation experts posit.

       ... rather that than wonder why words freeze
each time we touch
               or ask 'What is it?'
leaves us wooden, forked, apart.

Inattention

So much is wasted
and we sleep between. The good
wood desk was dark, deep waxed.
My nail file scrapes it
and digs out stain.

Or else this talking will
at once collapse. The cloud was
shifting. As we climbed the road,
the light that faded
would roll back again.

Now our discussions
must come to a point. My marginal
doodle is losing its curve. An
arrow-head forms at
the apex of pain.

Person: Tense and Number

Arrive in November and on the latest train
to walk through the brewery smells cutting
the river to the dead city centre. Then climb
a mile's light silence plus your shoes' echo
by Victorian growth up to newer suburbs. I've
other ways of approaching — "have had" — that
imitate a safe return, so that reaching the top
of the town is smoothly relaxing a grip.

"Was." With the early returns appropriated
and no investment forthcoming, it is lack now
dominates. Street corners exhale contextless
ghosts with guilt edging, that shiver and
embarrass. This place is consigned for memory.
Presence is of mind to sink in the capital among
the married mass, at professional parties
forgetting foundations. Formal. A face

that concerns itself with erasure, accretion
(so as to not lose face). It is taking a rhythm
from the underground: distortions of doubled
glass muddy it. It seeps into oligocene loam.
Weekends are escapes. The deep country dark
is desirable, playing the soundtrack from a
retreat. Reflection can be avoided. A mirror
and white walls is not what I asked for.

32°C

The Trident is doing its diagonal overhead drone
while an assortment of starlings makes scattering
manoeuvres about twilight. We sit on the stone steps.
It is high June and full heat that shocks newspapers
persists in still air. We are in gratitude for the day
and its prospect that seems to open on a street whose
trees are comfortable like wealth. Only at this close
a fluttering comes of faith, an itch, almost a gasp.

We are watching from a house out of the nineteenth
century, looking down from its steps on a garden we've
no strong wish to tend. The street we desire is in
shadow from this other street. The indifferent suburb,
where you sense indifference in a dull wash like
variations in car design or fashions of urban renewal,
is part of our unease and as large as bowel movements
or dry throbbing light in our reading of the day.

What feels like a gasp out of the nineteenth century,
a *let us be true to one another* flung in unbelief
at sea, signifies hope that small trusting creatures
can learn to share living. We touch to that rhythm
and glance indoors at the ephemera of love, collected.
We know something that the street has learned, if we
cannot know the street. While starlings return to
their wire, the Trident ends its long escaping roar.

March 19th 1977

Trying to get things right with terribly yellow
daffodils and the *Times* at Saturday breakfast,
so as to make it a leisurely morning where
hopes might sort our hours to harmonious
order. Decanting the frozen orange juice,
thinking of friends or having paid the
credit card bill; this is sufficiency. There
is sunlight on the fruit bowl as well.

A day for such carelessness. When someone
was crying on the end of the phone, you'd
think something was wrong with the line.
When friends come to dinner, you want more
wine and compliments on the moussaka
and would float through hearing anything
about it—how someone's life has turned so
grey with worry, nothing in him makes sense.

You would. But somehow the loves we have
make their terrible connections clear.
You do hear the weeping remember
what blankness is. You're there where
hopes fall on their face from mid-leap. It's like
bad news on the radio of the admired great
and worse and still you cannot help. If you
believed in God, he would have to explain all this.

Nos Meilleurs Clichés

The queues in the motorway cafés are moving
more slowly this summer; but there's a lot of
lively talk on the road to egg, sausage and beans.
An excitement has started as we head south,
dressed for the parallel life. This pause is the
arena of our anxious planning. We compute
forgotten supplies, check times of arrival
to tunes of pre-cooked food and corporate décor.

The papers are keeping us awake with cricket
victories or the death of Presley. They help our
digestions, until we are already glowing with
greedy thoughts of what we might bring back.
Me by Hotel X. Loved ones near the Prado.
Mountains and beaches are waiting in sunlight
for recording eyes and we will snap them up as
bargain backdrops for our self-display. We have

the scenes already framed and squared and
we are in them. Now the image we'll treasure
(what never quite happened) is prepared in the
heart. Something to meditate on in winter years,
against troubled children or lack of money. When
your best evenings are brought down to the language
of Rupert Murdoch. 'Look', you will say,
'the year of cricket and the death of Chaplin'.

[11]

The Strange Conversions

He opens the door: black shirt, black jeans. The day,
he says, has an affinity with black. The neutron bomb
is in his speech while a woman is reading fresh accounts
of rape. Knife wounds erupt in any smirk until a bolt and
chain is snapped across each opening of light. Their right
to fear closes the syllogism. A darkness in the rain
no conspiracy explains. Smashed lights at the pedestrian
crossing, supermarket trolleys abandoned like streets.

A corner in any Western city. Communist posters
slapped on the face of Sir 'Jimmy' Goldsmith, alternative
theatre in an unlikely pub. And on the end of a terrace
or unused wall the bright realist mural appears. Simplified
workers defy abstract bulldozers beneath cartoon cranes.
Near Pernety or Kentish Town the half-planned decades
collide in carnival. Optimists of agitprop rehearse in the
co-operative restaurant, waiting for their notice to quit.

The year is closing in and news of friends arrives.
The schoolboy radical joins the Ministry of Defence.
The born-again Christian contemplates adultery.
How they disappoint, these parodies of betrayal.
Like our own inaction, this lethargy
that fudges every act. Convictions cancelling
each other out until I cannot imagine change.
Only an empty planet, a passive mind erased.

Eden is Burning

after Masaccio

They are escaping. Or that is the story you
wish on us, as though a fresco were trying to be
human before the light killed it. It is their desire
we long for—though they grasp in despair, the
winning team home, their mouths dry and wordless.
We cannot be pure, my love. This is the suffering
of small nations, the tail of a continent
and 'people of whom we know nothing'.

We hide from our knowledge like the yellow press
plumping the stair carpet. We ignore the weak noise,
at night, of failing machinery. On paper it is
the same stale news, the unspeakable poetry.
I'm unhappy about the naked world with its
pictures of breasts above leopard skin.
Thin bodies again with ancient anxiety.
The new demands, the fishnets abandoned.

Too small a catch for any thought of victory.
Does the religious revival worry you, the
absent fuel of volition? Or those angry sectarians
in the kitchen garden? Something stays cooking.
The hi-fi plays on, in time to the breaking
crustaceans. It's foolish to run, to miss the long
perspective. Watch them pass us, with their
high colouring, their tragic touch of the human.

The Hypnopompic State

While no-one moves, the guards are slapping the small
arms strapped against their thighs. Behind is the sound
of migrating birds dying too early in border country. We rub
our eyes, hoping to dismiss the dim green threat of light.
Thinking of treacherous marshes we lie still, remembering
civilized synonyms for massacre. Always a shrike
is calling: the butcher-bird biding her time, like our
blue-eyed commander with her handshake and smiles.

Something from beyond the high wooden fences still
clings to our skin—more like bindweed than barbed wire.
We retain its sweating explanation of why we are here.
It comprehends the body's disposition—why our
limbs like to imitate certain plants, our eyes are only rested
by the intermittent light of an alien star.
Hearing that sound again, you turn to look at the hills
where the white rim of the radio telescope rotates.

It is listening to a world long beyond aided sight
or to the small deaths of ancient galaxies.
Our whispers in the dark seem strangely technical.
We've heard the shuddering playback of our selves,
the uncommitted crimes, the promises and planned
betrayals. Music is reconstituted in high trees like a
choking last breath. As though day might never begin,
a raw laughter is echoing—while no-one moves.

Impossible Object

Nothing quite as it seems. A clarity
to provoke curtains like dawn of
your longest day. It cannot compel
us to wake, or even jolt the shared
bed's little grip on trust. Before it is
time for words, we lose their touch.
We live in their aftertaste, nervously—
hearing the dream hangover, the muttering of news.

I am moving out of my love for you
into a new material city.
One of those days for travelling through
presents its tempting, expensive face.
All I can offer is foolish or used.
Let me trade that for the promises
I've sensed, liquid pleasures poured
from window-studded streets.

Gin-crazed at night, I thought
I would step down from the balcony
and hover higher than fear, holding
the warmth of a loving applause.
Morning is here like gravity. It's the
ordinary earth and fog like something
wrong with sight. I hear your nearness,
dearest voice, as light flickers off then on.

A Social Survey

There is more than you thought of
to the construction of reality.

The aspect of a window that
is prospect framed or white wood
boxing a sample world chivvies
at waiting, as a girl in the rain licks an
ice-cream, leaving the picture.

A house with a ladder propped
against it is opposite
and, visible through dust, remains.

Idealist

She wondered at the corner
to see them take away at last
the huge decaying elm.
It was the day she left for good
the rambling childhood home.

Sections of tree were chained to several lorries.
It stopped, as well as her, the traffic.

For months to come it's strange
to not return there.
In another district she imagines
the tree's great shadow
with her not there to see.

Against the Great

In these small streets
               not mean
it is the influence of avenues, you see.
We don't let narrowness
               worry us.
Turning magazine pages, we're various.

Look at the boys in their thirties
               admiring a dirty Buick.
Nothing hurts
in these small streets. The mean
is imitation-gilded, open-handed, clean.

Top Floor

Waking to the pleasant modern art
the walls of books, tasteful mementoes,
she looks down on the playground.
The boys smash wood and test fireworks in cans.
She looks down at them
tracking speechless movements from a distance
as if putting titles onto film.

But there are no stories
or too many to cohere
and she confuses them with one
forgotten before. *When she knew he'd left us
our mother drew us to her thighs and cried.*
The postcard had a picture of a ship.

Since then she's liked the view from distances,
learned to examine faces closely
and forget when they seem annoyed,
happy indifferent faces
unbaptised by fear.

A Model for Vermeer

Weighing the value of a time
in a dainty metal scale,
she holds it to the light
which is patient return to a tincture.

Meanwhile a man with a globe
is itching to get in on the act:
with compasses and maps,
the closed book, history.

Alison

In the big-framed window she is wiping,
I see a view like guide-book pictures:
the place, its abbey and antiquities.
This is not the day to view it. She shivers
as the rain falls steadily outside.

She is settling into marriage as the
winter settles into Bath. His clever
talk is not what she remembers. There
are noises where he hit her on the ear.

Free talk. Free love. Among the interference
she senses memories of sex, athletic,
like a comic muzak. Buzzes echo
a passionate frankness that went off key.

She is settling to marriage, accepting
with strange humour. She has wiped the glass
with patience. She wants to make it clean.

The Retreat

Washed clean of what we came here from,
the sky hangs tall above us. All around,
the knitted green of fields is flickering
with suggestions of wind, while our few
birds, like visitors, twitter about peace.

Why do you hide away from the world?
he asked. We hide from nothing, hear
cracks from pheasant guns or the
background buzz of crop-spraying planes.
Last night my mother rang with words

against our life like drumming hail.
If you want silence, the pine-padded floor
of the wood here should be quiet enough,
or evenings when we cannot speak
and moths are fighting in the paper shade.

Cousins

It is too much for him, suddenly too much.
Adding it up is too much; trying to make
ends meet in other people's lives is too much.
He wants the imagined comfortable room
where they all like him, and the sensible music.
Already someone is tuning a viola, but
the doorbell rings and he has to answer a letter.

The one you wouldn't mistake him for wakes
hungover and it's the crisis of capitalism.
Windows matter to him and dusty lino
edging round the room. He wants
the radio that bugs him and cigarettes
to numb him in the itching day. His headache
stretches out, spoiling the possible.

Each is the other's problem.
I see them in a street of tall houses.
They will not admit they're relations.

On the Beach

Encountering the flotsam
of words, eager
and curious, searching
the individual stone,
I lost the predictable curve
of gulls in still air,
mislaid the familiar,
the obvious coastline.

It is broken bottles
and the accidents of sun
make up the green lights
we mistake for growth;
and only the high-voiced wind
heard whistling above
attaches our focus
to the colourless day

—the day colour is drained from,
whose treasure of words
wind and the waiting sea
wear down to dry stone.

The Old Worship

On Station Road the rockabilly fans cradling loud
cassette players slouch with brutal authority like
connoisseurs of art. You arrive with a standard-
lamp and flowers in your hat. My druid priestess.
It is Saturday in the tiresome world — too late to
start a religion. We make our way along a pavement
crowded with difficulty: unsure who is still
friendly to us, whom we should pretend to love.

There is the library to be comfortable in when
your thoughts chatter. Hear the microprint index
whirr. It flies through an orchard of shelves,
their branches heavy with cling-film coloured fruit.
Maybe today there will be something new. My
shining notes glitter in their ache for synthesis.
Beyond the modern glass, the car park with its
new thin trees waits respectfully for spring.

Or perhaps there is sorting our furniture again,
moving the carpet we are not tired of, getting
a fresh hold on the room. Then we will be ready
for the cosy months, the long days we take refuge
in. There will be time for sacred music and time for
distractions. Hope for that. Let us ignore the
brown packet of letters, the unfamiliar hand,
the old thin words of those we have failed to love.

Above Genoa

It's from a dream this landscape and I'm waiting
for some ghost of mine to jump. I know the way
it feels when floating out, the gasp at missing
jutting rocks, the trees, how long it seems to take
to reach the mindless grey. The laughter in thin air.
But here the evidence of work as well, this solid life
spent building into hills. Even this blue water
looks real as history, as hopeful in its wealth.

And it's the real world we're walking in, where
you can read novels about fucking and despise
how words decay. We climbed here by funicular
but, on the road, teenagers lift the throttles of
their Vespas to a pitch of monstrous dialectic.
Look, inland to where the new roads cut the valley,
or, where the land resists, break rock. Follow
with your eye commerce, its graceful directives.

It must be the air or the early sunshine but there
are lungfuls of hope inside me in spite of all this.
I came for the view that's inside me where cities
run their smooth affairs like a socialist bus,
where work is a kindly system of barter
and every cheese has flavour. I am happy
where the horizon is indistinct and news in
another language. This is quite unlike a dream.

In Genoa

The paired stars click in place between the tall
pillars of Principe station. Three hours of delay
while the black-cassocked clerks in the left-luggage
office nod out an inquisition's civility. Where
history is an ignored background, a peeling
eighteenth-century façade sprayed in violent
black or red, bargains still have to be made,
resentments sharpened on a lifetime's edge of steel.

You could believe Jessica stole her mother's ring
for a monkey here. A boy whittles a block of wood,
listening to pirated tapes near the unlikely house
of Columbus. Across the alley, a spare black dog
shifts his autonomous haunches from a huge, upended
turd. We walk ahead, admiring mysterious local
funghi—while old women shout out their contempt
looking beyond us with tough detached disgust.

That window, halfway up the scratched stained plaster lets
in a little light at noon, a little bitter chatter.
A breeze just kind enough for a generous thought.
A smashed guitar by the wall or the poems of Brecht.
This is where the heart has stored its few possessions,
maintained its strange attempt at unpossessive love.
The blinds are open for the street's words, as if he
expected 'the simple thing—so difficult to achieve'.

'His best piece of poetrie'

His face in the cot is his great-grandmother's face.
The face his mother places in a frame downstairs
retains his anxious smile. In that brown-mottled
photograph, a woman sits on the awkward edge
of a bentwood chair. She wears a Regency-striped dress
the son who barely knew her remembers as blue. Her fur-trimmed
coat will not take off the chill of fear, as she looks out to us —
who taste the times she did not live to understand.

Tigris and Suir, Tawe and the Manchester Ship Canal.
Will he see the waters where his elders wept?
Innocent of thought, Sam gurgles in his sleep, a blue
tortoise rising on his slowcoach moving chest.
Armenians in Baghdad before a genocidal war; Irish
impatient for their dignity. Those who fled their patriarchs
or misers for a small secure success, for England's late
complacency — migrate to his quiet breath and heart.

When he comes of age in quite another century,
what will he think of them among what other sorrows?
From the dark future he'll look back at someone
else's dream. A dream of all the centuries — and we
who wish him only joy may not be wise enough to grasp
its meaning. I feel the grip of the dear hand that circles
my small finger. As strong as hope. And think about
Ben Jonson's words, his child who died at seven.

Night Shift

after Le Travail du Poète *by Phillipe Jaccottet*

We're like night-watchmen,
our eyes more salmon-red
at each hour's end, but not
from crying or a dream's
disturbance—we're pastors
naming every item left at risk,
all to be lost should sleep
disturb our husbandry.

Fading Chameleons

No longer invisible,
you can tell us
from other lizards
by old habits of our vocation

Abandoned wizardry
and too-long lingering eyes,
chafed articulation,
worn, inappropriate clothes

Contre-jour
(portraits of Ezra Pound)

that mastery of ink and brush
       the chisel's grave hierarchy
           accepted
but Avedon's photograph
       6.30.58
             Rutherford New Jersey
cut citrus sun-dried
       a thin shirt draped
             on the coarse cloth skin
they saved for him
       sore lips threatening speech
             the Titan's loose robe
without Kent or Cordelia
       the eyelid's sewn purse
             holding something back
or shut against too much light

At Laugharne

From the stilted boathouse
a narrow window opens
to the broad grey stretch of sea
he answered carelessly.

The pale peeled paint
of his writing shed fades
and the staggering boasts
of one who fell for words
'to beat them now and then'
rebound on the distant spray.

'Balloons'

Kennedy's promise
to 'put a man on
the moon—and bring
him back' or is it
the harmonica break
in *Love me Do*?

Anything with 1963
written under it
rather than a February
room in Primrose Hill
with snow six weeks old
still crackling and stiff.

She moves between two
children and a typewriter,
noticing those oval,
brightly coloured moons
of air; stepping closer to
the crackling lunar edge.

Household Words

for Peter Robinson

The advertising business is about you today.
Certain investments have brought your name to our attention
and well qualified individuals have decided the lettering.
You exist as a design for carrier bags
and a reputation for quality.

I know the embarrassment of names,
suffering notoriety young thanks to Lonnie Donegan.
Only recently
the voice of someone's mother called from four floors up:
'Tim, behave yourself!'

I must make an attempt.
I try to dress like someone involved in a serious game,
but it's hard to make words settle down
to a serious career in marketing.
They are everywhere like uncared-for children.

There is a dream of words at peace with themselves,
lying together under glass
in the imaginary museum.
'Stringency' 'luxuriates'
and you cannot hear a sound.

Mine shuffle along mismatched shelves,
come from under the bed like battered shoes.
The cracked radio spits them out
—orphan words
and more are coming from the street outside.

The Page

You liked it at the beginning,
then it was so many promises:
new colours of cloth and unexpected tastes.
Now they have names like Paisley or Pizza Sorpresa.
They remind you of Ulster or long delays in the post.
It was so easy with the old coinage
—something given like a climate,
your options an experimental art.
Everywhere you hope for a skyline
wiped clear of freezing sun,
affection offering her balcony
lifting you into the clear.
As if it had ever happened,
as if you woke one morning to a midsummer dawn
that offered itself as a stage
on which you were dancing and lovely.
You want to have a way with words and an audience
that smiles.
Now the possible pasts accuse you instead,
the conversations fuzzy and full of regret.
What you could not decide
works inside like a malignant root.
It demands the places you're forgetting,
the fresh page with its horrible white.
It is tunnelling towards you with corridors
you run along.
I hear breathing like delight.
You will not like the end.

A Forbidding Spring

There's nothing charming
about rain on a March Saturday, or a family breakfast
with attention divided
between window and room—forgetting one's words
to focus for a moment
on daffodils that look in at us, soaking and hurt,
or a single item of news.

I'm beginning to panic
about messages that remain unheard, legal silencings.
Notes pass from hand to hand
to be lost unaccountably; letters are damaged in transit.
Or those who pass words on
are damaged unaccountably; their movements limited.
The whistleblower's jailed.

The tunnels are policed.
'When the cat goes off, the rhythm of steel on concrete.
Against the fact of torture,
we imagine a truth in the other prisoners' lies.'
When word of such words
leaks out, it is the occasion of arrest and exile.
We've yet to know the worst.

Today it is only rain.
They don't tell us what was said at night, how
the classified cables
have tied our tongues, twisting the torque
of what's not said in love.
'I can't tell a joke with the new forms of speech
still less write a poem.'

[36]

Can his poem outlive
the leader he'd attack? The innocent in office
        posts an incriminating file.
Our friends are preparing for the great march
        to the old town square.
Will we join them this year? Or is it time
        to send the polite reply
that blames an awkward age, or the forbidding weather?

Woman Reading

Dark green chenille, I think, hangs
half over the cupboard drawer
and your few 'precious things'
—that piece of jade, a lamp,
nothing contemporary—
weigh down the corner in a crowd of detail.
I see you from behind,
leaf-filtered light striking a neck
white as the book's slim vee.
It feeds you—perching on one hand,
perplexing, silent bird—
like memory, or deep orange ochre
in the postcard that marks a page.

In that early study, you confront
torched mines and noisy factories . . .
troubles wide and dark . . . an easy wheel
that sets sharp racks at work,
cold college rooms, persistent literature
that sets the heart's intents
to thought and struggle: banners red
as Keats's warm expectorated blood.

The later work
has you across from me;
an angled arm supports
your sleepy head and papers lie
along a table tangent to your chair.
A pierglass takes the light
and throws your tessellated profile out,
scarlet and black, knee over thigh,
in modern dress. A dream continuing
beneath flowers, framed photographs.

A terrible childbed hast thou had,
my dear. At rest, this evening,
you turn to Pericles' persistence,
to scenes where women's words
changed stubborn destinies.

Against a background of black,
your mind still turns on words,
still hoping to uncover
some complex source of light.

Heat Haze

These summer days suddenly thick with heat
call out for iced coffee and a memory of 1970:
London is waking behind sore eyes, assuming
the form of a courtyard in the Wallace Collection.
I'd left the solid air, the mercy-numbing noise
to meet Pieter de Hooch for the first time,
watching a corridor of light stretch to eternity.

The undeniable voice, with its elegant sparrowy
tone, told its companion: *England is finished.*
Returned from the Algarve, *Respect is ending.*
It's the same in Spain. They know the old men
will go and look beyond one. We'll see it go.
In Greece at least discipline can be relied on.
Angry at the undeniable, thirteen years on,
would my voice sound as shrill and stark?
The warmth of June, the election result,
so much bad temper and distrust,
our eyes and ears seem ill-informed.

Trying to work, I look about the room.
A child's distracting voice calls me out of thought.
He holds a tennis ball like offered fruit.
And suddenly I see the scenes as one:
the boy's small form framed by the garden door,
a figure inside called from daily tasks
by tennis ball or fruit, by distant light,
as if the promise offered by that child
the moments called to being by his voice
broke through the chequered limits of these days.

Yesterday,
light like this caught a three-foot profile
on the green canal
as my son stopped to listen on our walk and said,
he heard two things:
the bird's expected music in the trees and,
what I'd not heard,
our shoesteps crashing through the new crisp leaves.

Disturbance

Responsible authority
looks into thefts of
bandages and bottles.

At the word *agitation*
my hands begin to tremble
like someone made to speak.

Breakdown

It must be the longest time I've spent
in Lancashire. Fingernails touch-type
formica as we see through flecked glass
a prune and cream bus on a bridge.

The roofless mills: Nelson like Rievaulx.
A man about my age says that green swathe
by the canal bank was factories once.
Bare ruination. The train refuses to begin.

The South

The popular songs
of our language stress the
difference of this borderline.
Below the Rio Grande on
the peripheral freeway of
the world's largest city, she
changes down dawdling
behind the shaky *camión*
longer than she'd thought it
would take to notice
the fragile covering of skin,
the dead shanks rattling
outside the tarpaulin.
In Africa she'd left her
camera in the hotel, offering
no offence to the remnant
of a shirt, six pieces of fruit
or single row of nuts
arranged for market day.
In postmodern Middlesex,
vernacular brick and
glass stained brown watch
a wind disturb the stray
image of limbs trapped by
fallen plaster, the paper-
thin coverage of the shy
Nyala. A man in ageing
tweeds offers three suits
on a rail. A jukebox leaks
Mi amor, mi corazón.

Theale Churchyard

The lightest touch of wind
      that parts the leaves of grass
      along the level moor,
or lets us hear a latch
      tapping the casement glass
      that's left an inch ajar,
is eloquent enough.

The light moves slowly up
      the hills across from us
      while cattle feed beneath.
In deeper silence here,
      beside his little grave
      we have small use for speech
missing an absent breath.

The Rod

He leans toward
green water, precisely
deep as a strong
navigator's take.
His out-tray's
virgulae fidget
as Old Holborn fumes
divert midges.

His territorial
camouflage
trousers—like
the silvered radio
that trumpets
memories of feeling
much younger than this
—disguise nothing.

Young women
at lock-gates,
fresh as their
narrow-boat's
geranium windows
or bicycled roof,
attract his straitened
eye's sudden reproof.

He wishes he'd bribed
the grubby swans
away with bread
and looks at water
resembling itself,
— each rupture
in the brink
a glint of meaning.

His generous jaw
tightens to passion.
He'd abandon law
to own a stretch
of the Test, to sit
relaxed and watch
policemen in pairs
garden his privacy.

1948 (Elephant and Castle)

Loosening
my tie, in sudden autumn heat,
I look again
at this photograph from forty
years ago
I found on a postcard rack
last Saturday.

Soft-slippered feet resting
on the sill,
as a woman turns her cheek
against his
check-shirt shoulder, waiting
for some kind
word from him, smoking silent
beside her.

Thick white china, a rationed
hunk of fat,
fill the small utility table.
As she looks
in his eyes and he past hers,
the young hurt
faces hold something fragile,
like pre-war
building between them again.

For a moment,
I hear the spray on Southend pier,
            tight young steps
turning to walk back the length of it:
            faces smiling
as if to brave the years' slow
            count of loss,
their long garnering of storm.

The Apiarists

Beneath the gauze, his lips
are licked tight
on a message sealed long ago,
folded over and turned down
like the rejection of a smile.

His short chin is propped up
by fleshy rings of neck;
everything else in his face
is on the point of collapse
—except the gaze:

intent on the Fancy,
the proceedings of the convention.
He prepares a stinging comment
on the organization's honour,
its insufficient rules.

His co-delegate
wears a striped hat
from which black ringlets fall.
He is here for the buzz
of debate, the company

of workers in his field
and will not complain
if the lecture drones on half an hour
past schedule. He is young.
It's his first time here.

He's growing a beard.
Who is there to tell him
how his passion can harden
to a dark and sticky
concentration of cells?

For a Country Churchyard

Hearing in birdsong the twittering ice-cream bell,
at evening, out at the end of a line. Now
all the electric world from Iclenham to Blake Hall
is ignored in the allotment of peace. The field
full of pylons murmurs with grazing contentment.
Darkness comes slowly and the slow bells ring
from the church that alone outlasts this estate.

Someone is practising a change that resists all
new intrusion. Graveyard weeds hang on between
the iron railings and broken slabs. *Hodie mihi:
Cras tibi.* The inscription survives in damaged
confidence. Around it insects mutter and creak
insistent like a song about old liberties.

Network

Coming outdoors in autumn
$\qquad\qquad$ is to feel
the cold surprise of nature.
$\qquad\qquad\qquad$ First the black
of it with wailing trees,
$\qquad\qquad\qquad$ then rain's attack
through outer clothes and shirt to skin.

Electric-lit indoors
$\qquad\qquad\qquad$ seems less than real.
The trembling window glass
$\qquad\qquad\qquad$ repeats the storm.
A woman pulls the curtain to,
$\qquad\qquad\qquad$ and treasured warm
is sealed defensively within.

I think it was against this the map was made.
I have its patterns in mind now.
I sense the different coloured lines,
$\qquad\qquad$ the multiple connections.
It is like a complex piece of surgery
$\qquad\qquad$ or a painting by Mondrian.
It is obscurely comforting.

It is the web of caring:
$\qquad\qquad\qquad$ its lines reveal
our effort and intention;
$\qquad\qquad\qquad$ its every link
extends thin wires of hope.
$\qquad\qquad\qquad$ Do not think, now.
Begin to trace the fragile threads. Begin.

Tidying Up

Yesterday, an hour of daylight left,
we cut our losses, knowing not much would be achieved.
You settled an old bill. I dug a hole
ready to replant the Christmas tree. Then together
we lifted the wet fencing that had fallen on the lawn
and humped it down the garden to lean against
the shed. I looked back at the pale latticed square
the fence had left, straw-coloured, circled by flies.
I watched you walk back in the house and turn
to see me watching still. I wedged the sodden
wood behind a line of bricks, careful
of the dank and naked hawthorn to one side.

Upstairs, once it was already dark,
you found your brooch was missing from your blouse.
You almost mourned the tapestry cameo and its metal
Victorian frame, fallen somewhere to grass. This morning,
feeling how much less of loss I know than you,
I poked in the black mulch around the evergreen
and scanned the struggling grasses without luck.
Carelessly, I emptied the old dustbin that had filled
with rain of a McEwan's can, a Mickey Mouse shoe-bag,
and—in a shock of grey and white—this still fresh squirrel
that must have slipped and drowned.

So I had to dig another hole
in a patch where nothing much would grow,
remembering as I edged the pale belly on the spade
a scampering through autumn to the pile of nuts,
acorns mostly, that our children had gathered
nearby. Other squirrels may come to the garden;
that tree may well take root. I hope
we find your brooch or another like it;
but however carefully we watch each other,
your mother and your father won't come back.

Without Compulsion

Conning
the list
of books
no longer recommended
by the fiction committee

and taking
note of
the latest
instructions on
compulsory pleasure

I resort to the public park.

My sportswear is a shade different
than the regulation colours
(Damned lavomat ideographs!)

The sun doesn't have to shine
and the book with the brown paper cover
may be *Jane Eyre*
or *Biggles Goes East.*

40th Birthday with Cassette Deck and Questions

In the next room children come and go,
talking of Michelangelo
and other awesome dudes.
O'Driscoll is on his knees again,
deciding which cut of *One Too Many Mornings*
to dub for the party tapes.

Is that a smell of burning?

He settles for an upbeat country treatment
from the Isle of Wight bootleg.
The blue-jeaned tolerant original
they'd be embarrassed by. And he's not ready yet
for the leather-coated stand-off of *Hard Rain*.

Should he risk a white suit?

Beginning a slow bowler's windmill
to ease his stiff shoulder,
he remembers a song of Pete Townshend's.
The line *I was just 34 years old.*

Will anybody come?

Memory

The Half Moon stood on its own,
somewhere to the left of the
city-centre roundabout, in what,
after more than thirty years away,
part of me still wants to call my
home town. In 1968 (or 9?), I saw
Mississippi Fred McDowell
play there, in an upstairs room.

Bottleneck blues, its dips and slides.
Railroad rhythms, high pizzicato
cries; the keening
of pressured strings, a voice
under the voice that spoke
as much as sang—wading through
water with the name Booker T.
Washington—*if the river was
whiskey and I was a diving duck,
Lord, I would dive on the bottom.
Baby, and I would never come up.*

In the interval, McDowell had
rested his unwhiskey-carrying
hand on my right shoulder while
pale local talent played. He was
more than sixty then, thin-armed
with hardened working hands.
He'd driven tractors, planted cornrows
and, weekends,
made music
in kitchens (sometimes
juke-joints) to please friends
who sometimes paid.

As it was Sunday, in the second set
we gave some time *to the Lord*.
Razor chords he'd copied first
from an uncle who played open tuning
with a big bone out of a steak.
Then, *Oh well, Don't you be un-
easy, Don't you be uneasy, Don't
you be uneasy, Jesus gonna make up
my dy*. . . . The last two syllables
swallowed in music. My dying bed.

The Other

If I said the man
sitting on the bench
in the churchyard
was talking to himself,
this would not be the truth.

The man I saw as I stopped
by the traffic lights
on Wealdstone High Street
at about 10.40 a.m.
on a surprisingly bright
Wednesday in November.

The man with the trilby hat,
the herringbone overcoat
one size too big, and a smart-
seeming scarf in a shade
you might call damson,
was not talking to himself.

He addressed, with animation,
a point at eye-level,
eighteen inches away
from the unshaven chin,
the damson scarf.

His eyes moved quickly,
intelligently, persuasively even,
as he addressed the absence
eighteen inches away
from his blue-veined nose.

He had the air
of a man about to grasp
his invisible companion,
to embrace him,
to explain again to him
there was nothing to fear.

Tact

Unannounced, you sidled
rather than stumbled
into this dream of a blazing
family row. Sitting it out
modestly, looking not unembarrassed
at my performance, moving
your clenched broad fingers
between one another, flexing them
in a gesture between exasperation
and prayer.
          My hectoring voice
wavers as you look abashed at me,
like that skateboarder halting suddenly,
as the hearse climbed the hill to your last
view of the lighthouse and the pier.

You didn't speak, but sat,
an unobtrusive visitor.
Your wild white hair, your moustache
like crests of foam, looking
—not neatly combed and stiff
as we saw them in the chapel of rest—
but as I saw you last alive,
guiding my fledgling driver's eye
to the parking space by the hospital doors.

Or more than twenty years before,
after the last great flare of adolescence,
waking early and without rancour
to drive me to the station and my friends.
Or earlier still, on the day of my sister's birth,
calming us into the car, with words
of the love sons owe to mothers and warnings
against taking sides.

              Which quieten
my raised voice now, accustom me
to the long and patient view
over a perturbed and placid-seeming bay
where, without you, I must learn
your watchful, unassertive gift.

Working from Home

Watching, through the open
French doors and conservatory glass, these birds queuing
    at the feeder, pecking
and spitting out nuts and seeds, submissively anointing
    their forefeathers
in the drinking bowl, I tidy a table, content with
    what's brought us here:
times of waiting or worry, or losing our patience,
    and days like these
when someone takes the children out and someone stays
    with papers to read.
One day you're at the wave-pool. Spread out on the floor
    are coursework folders:
teenage fiction, research on street-gangs, someone's response
    to Wesker's *Roots*
and Hamid's painful, broken story of escaping from Tehran.
    Shootings, disappearances,
a Pepsi Cola lorry overturned, unclean, its sticky bubbly fluid
    running in the streets.
Another day you're working. In the Science Museum
    Sam, Benedict and I
start the combine harvester, make counterweights for bridges
    or launch a rocket.
Inside one case an Edsel; further on the crooked foot-digger
    Hebridean crofters
called a caschcrom. By raising or lowering a handle,
    those too poor to plough
determined the depth of the groove they needed to cut
    in the sparse soil,
then gripped the wooden shaft and kick-started the share.

I was writing some review
that Saturday you and the children went to London Zoo.
                Waiting in line
for llama rides, you thought you recognised the smiling, neat
                and prematurely balding man
holding his son's hand just ahead, steadying him in the cart.
                It turned out not to be,
you realised on the train coming home, another parent
                from the local school,
but the man who'd won the Booker Prize for *Midnight's Children*.
                Now you're upstairs
writing a reference for a nurse in your Literature class,
                while I chop onions
and listen for our not quite warring sons. Though
                the author of *Shame*
might fear to be seen with a child in public and the enclosing,
                impoverishing mind
shouts 'Kill the Ba'hais' or plans forced migrations, at evening
                perennial birdsong
brightens our garden. It doesn't make everything right, but
                makes it easier,
the children bathed and read to, easier to touch another's hand,
                or speak quietly,
so when night does come what we notice is an arc of moonlight
                curved by the ribbed
plastic roof above us—no rainbow or triumphal arch, but
                what work tends toward—
efforts of love: attention, desire, holding darkness at bay.

Nightfall

Throughout autumn, all through the graduated,
creeping grey of journeys past the railway bridge,
    Lucille noted days on which
    light kept its promises—great
      blocks of pale or darker blue
offset by russets, lemons or maroons.
Businesses thrived or closed. Beggars sang tunes
or sold cheap lighters. She watched the sky for change
until it seemed she reached the end of change.

Darkening days lit up with festivals,
fireworks for Diwali or Guy Fawkes.
    Week-ends meant shorter, damper walks,
    or trips to newly opened malls
      outside the city limits.
This week new Beaujolais. All the next,
displays of party dresses. Under lights,
in air-warmed atria, she felt as if on stage,
as if what haunted her was just a stage

to pass through like the others. Winter colds
hung on longer than before. Foggy air
    left stains on the windscreen of her car.
    All of it made her feel old
      suddenly. Outside, an
ear-ringed, peak-capped boy played *Nowhere Man*,
his dog wrapped in a neat plaid blanket. And
Happy Christmas (War is Over) played again
in the lift to the parking floors. And again

small nations' griefs plumped up the weekend press.
Each widow's grief was different and the same.
     Each mother's horror measured as
     a fractured smile, a face undressed.
          Lucille put on her mask,
set out to face the early evening's tasks,
thought again how much the year had asked
of her. At the street's end stood the sky:
the overbearing, weighty, hardened sky.

The dashboard LCD read 16:12.
Tall orange streetlights started to come on.
     Behind them, sulphurous yellow ran
     its course beneath the groaning shelf
          of cloud that thickened still.
Is this how dark it gets? The question Lucille
asked could penetrate the crystalline array
of solid surfaces, enter a space
an angstrom wide, or reach to distant space,

interrogating emptiness of galaxies,
asking non-decreasing event horizons
     what light comes in or out. Reasons,
     arguments—the stuff exegesis
          explores—implode near
a black hole's neither light nor darkened door;
and interstellar spaces no longer hoard
a crown of candles, or some freakish star.
Lucille looked at the clouded night which no star

burst through. Inside houses, coloured balls
cheered wrecked conifers, families found meaning
   in games or company. Nothing
    egregious disturbed decked halls.
     Lucille dropped out of sight.
Without her, little changed. The sky grew lighter
a little longer as the year turned. White
petals broke the soil's crust — the grave of all
kept its secrets . . . almost like nothing at all.

Lightning Source UK Ltd.
Milton Keynes UK
07 January 2011
165325UK00001B/26/P